RIVER FOREST PUBLIC LIBRARY

3 1865 00158 6733

W9-ARD-651

12051x LC1105

RIVER FOREST PUBLIC LIBRARY
735 Lathrop Avenue
River Forest, Illinois 60305
708 / 366-5205

6/05

$27

HABITATS
Tropical Rainforests

Robert Snedden

RIVER FOREST PUBLIC LIBRARY
735 LATHROP
RIVER FOREST, IL 60305

Smart Apple Media

Published by Smart Apple Media
2140 Howard Drive West, North Mankato, Minnesota 56003

Designed by Helen James

Photographs by Corbis (Brandon D. Cole, Jay Dickman, Michael & Patricia
Fogden, Galen Rowell, Kevin Schafer), Jay Ireland & Georgienne Bradley, JLM
Visuals (Richard P. Jacobs), Tom Stack & Associates (Chip & Jill Isenhart, Mark
Newman, Brian Parker, Inga Spence, Mark Allen Stack, Tom & Therisa Stack,
TSADO/NASA, Dave Watts, Tess & David Young)

Copyright © 2005 Smart Apple Media. International copyrights reserved in all
countries. No part of this book may be reproduced in any form without written
permission from the publisher.

Printed in the USA

Library of Congress Cataloging-in-Publication Data

Snedden, Robert.
Tropical rainforests / by Robert Snedden.
p. cm. — (Habitats)
Includes index.
Contents: Where are the rainforests? — Rainforest weather — Living in layers
— Rainforest recycling — Life at ground level — Understory life — Top of the
trees — Tree climbers — Monkeying around — Apes of the forest – A multitude of
minibeasts — Hunters of the forest — The threatened forest.
ISBN 1-58340-382-5
1. Rain forests—Juvenile literature. 2. Rain forest ecology—Juvenile
literature. [1. Rain forests. 2. Rain forest ecology. 3. Ecology.] I.
Title.

QH86.S565 2004
577.34–dc21   2002042814

First Edition

9 8 7 6 5 4 3 2 1

Contents

Where Are the Rainforests?

The place where a living thing makes its home is called its **habitat**. A habitat can be as small as a damp place under a rotting log, or as big as the ocean. The biggest habitats, such as deserts, forests, and mountains, are called **biomes**.

Finding the forest

Forest biomes cover large areas of Earth's land. There are several different kinds of forest biomes. One kind, the tropical rainforest, circles the planet around its middle like a green belt. Tropical rainforests are found in places where the temperatures are always high and where a lot of rain falls throughout the year. Close to the

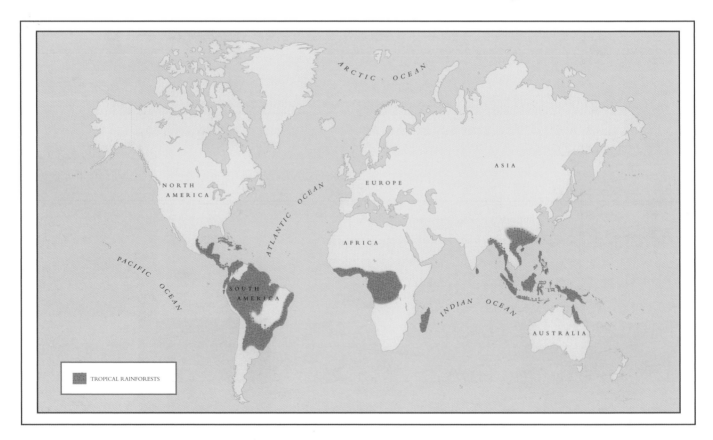

*Tropical rainforests form a green band around the **equatorial** regions of Earth.*

equator, in Asia, Africa, and Central and South America, the conditions are right for tropical rainforests to grow.

The largest rainforest in the world grows around the Amazon River in South America. It alone makes up almost half of the world's rainforest habitat. In Africa, rainforests grow around the Congo River of West Africa and near the coast of the Atlantic Ocean. There is also a rainforest on the east coast of the island of Madagascar. The rainforests of Asia are found in two main areas. One area includes Malaysia, the islands of Borneo, and the Philippines. The other covers large areas of the island of New Guinea and parts of northern Australia.

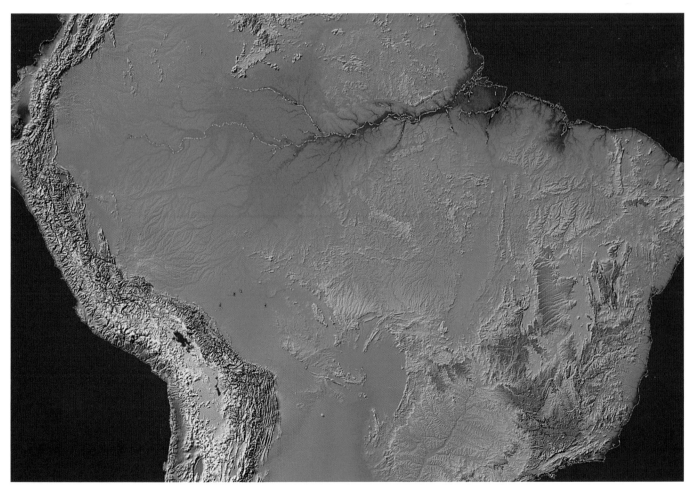

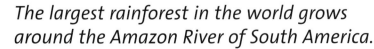

The largest rainforest in the world grows around the Amazon River of South America.

5

Rainforest Weather

On a typical day in a rainforest, the weather is likely to be hot and steamy. The temperature doesn't change much over the course of the year near the equator. It rarely falls below a warm 68 °F (20 °C) and doesn't often get above 93 °F (34 °C).

▲ *Leaves on rainforest trees have pointy "drip-tips" to help water run off them.*

Elfinwoods

Because the temperature drops as **altitude** increases, true rainforests are not found above 3,300 feet (1,000 m). High on tropical mountains, the trees are small and covered by mosses and ferns. These woods are called elfinwoods, or cloud forests, and are like rainforests in miniature.

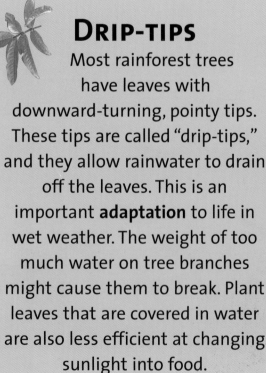

DRIP-TIPS

Most rainforest trees have leaves with downward-turning, pointy tips. These tips are called "drip-tips," and they allow rainwater to drain off the leaves. This is an important **adaptation** to life in wet weather. The weight of too much water on tree branches might cause them to break. Plant leaves that are covered in water are also less efficient at changing sunlight into food.

Vast amounts of water evaporate from the leaves of rainforest trees.

Wet, wet, wet!

There are no dry seasons in a true rainforest. It is wet year-round. As little as 80 inches (200 cm) or as much as 350 inches (900 cm) of rain might fall over the course of a year. Usually, at least eight inches (20 cm) of rain will fall every month in a rainforest. By comparison, even the wettest parts of rainy Great Britain rarely see more than 60 inches (150 cm) of rain in a year.

Living weather machines

Half of the rain that falls on the Amazon rainforest blows in from the Atlantic Ocean. The rest is produced by the trees of the forest. Trees are like giant, living water pumps, bringing up moisture from the ground. This moisture is lost through the leaves of the trees by **evaporation**. The moist air from the trees' leaves rises up above the forest. When it hits colder air, the rising moist air forms clouds, and the water falls back to the earth as rain.

Living in Layers

Like a multi-storied apartment building, the rainforest is divided into different layers. Each layer has its own distinctive characteristics and tenants.

Life at the top

Standing proudly above the forest **canopy** are the emergent trees—the giants of the forest. They have massive trunks more than seven feet (2 m) across and reach heights of 115 to 230 feet (35-70 m) or more. The emergents are widely spaced and have umbrella-shaped tops. Fast-flying birds and bats swoop between the treetops.

Up on the roof

The trees that form the canopy of the rainforest grow from 70 to 100 feet (20-30 m) tall. They have dense, leafy crowns, or tops, that absorb most of the sunlight, preventing it from reaching the layers below. Vast numbers of animals make their homes in the canopy.

*Flowers in the rainforest are **pollinated** by a variety of insects, animals, and birds, including hummingbirds. Without these creatures, many plants could not reproduce.* ▼

emergent trees

canopy

understory

forest floor

▲ *Many different types of trees grow in the rainforest, forming distinct layers. Emergent trees stand out above the canopy below.*

Going down

The next level down is the understory. It is very damp and warm, with very little light. The plants that grow in the understory have very large leaves to collect as much light as possible. Understory trees tend to be about 30 to 50 feet (10-15 m) tall. The crowns of the trees are tightly packed together, but growth is sparse below, and animals can move easily between the trees. Flowers in the understory are brightly colored and have strong scents. These adaptations allow them to attract insects, birds, and bats in the dim light.

Ground floor

The ground level of a tropical rainforest is also warm, damp, and dark. The air is still. Unlike the environment portrayed by some jungle movies, there is little plant life on the rainforest floor. It is only on the edge of the forest or along the banks of rivers that enough light gets through for a lot of plants to grow.

Leaves and animal droppings from the layers above drop down to the forest floor. There they rot quickly and are consumed, or eaten, by huge numbers of ants, termites, and other minibeasts. In a short time, a rich **compost** forms, providing **nutrients** that are taken up by the many tree roots.

Rainforest Recycling

Rainforests look like incredibly **fertile** places. There is more living material in a square mile of rainforest than there is in the same space in any other habitat. However, even though the forest is very productive, it actually grows on very poor soil. Rainforest soils can't hold nutrients in the same way that soils in cooler climates can. High temperatures and heavy rainfall remove the nutrients from the soil. So, the question is, how do rainforests manage to grow so well?

Because most of the nutrients in a rainforest are stored within the trees, clearing the forest soon makes the land unproductive.

Little helpers

The high temperatures of the rainforest floor provide ideal growing conditions for bacteria. These microscopic organisms are among the rainforest trees' most important helpers. Any leaves, animal droppings, or other materials falling to the floor from the trees above are swiftly consumed by ants and other small animals. This is the first step in the rainforest **recycling** process. The bacteria then continue the process begun by

STILT SUPPORTS

Because rainforest trees have such shallow roots, they often have other means of support. Some trees have "stilt roots" that split off from the tree a few feet above the ground. These roots not only make the tree more stable, but they also allow the tree to obtain more nutrients from the soil. Other trees have large outgrowths at the base, called buttresses, that spread the weight of the tree out over a larger area.

Some rainforest trees have "stilt roots" to give them extra support.

the minibeasts. Together, they rapidly break down the leaves and other remains. In this way, the bacteria release the nutrients locked up in the droppings and make them available for the trees to use again.

The trees and the bacteria need each other to survive. The trees provide a source of food for the bacteria in the form of falling leaves, and the bacteria break the leaves down to provide the nutrients upon which the trees depend.

Tree stores

In the cooler forests of **temperate climates**, trees can take nutrients as they need them from the soil. In the rainforest, however, trees must compete with each other for nutrients as well as light. Rainforest trees have shallow roots that spread out over a wide area, unlike the deeply growing roots of temperate forest trees. Rainforest tree roots grab nutrients from the soil as soon as they become available, storing them in the living bodies of the trees.

11

Life at Ground Level

Because there is little plant growth at ground level in the rainforest, there is little for plant-eating animals to eat. Most are small- to medium-sized animals that feed on fruits and seeds that fall to the ground. Big **mammals** are far less common in the rainforest because of the lack of food, but there are a few. Examples include the elephants of Africa and Asia, the pygmy hippo and the gorilla of Africa, and the tapir of South America.

Little collectors

In rainforests all over the world, there are animals that feed on nothing but fallen fruits and seeds. The African rainforests are home to small antelopes called duikers. There are several varieties of duikers. Each kind is adapted to feed on a unique type of seed or fruit. One kind of duiker has teeth that can crack the hardest seed. Another has a flexible jaw that allows it to eat some of the largest fruits.

The blue duiker of Africa is one of the world's smallest antelopes, standing less than 16 inches (40 cm) tall at the shoulder.

Agoutis are cat-sized rodents that live in the rainforests of South America. These seed collectors perform a valuable service for the rainforest trees. They collect seeds and hide them to be eaten later. Often, the seeds are not eaten at all. Instead, they **germinate**, thanks to the animals, far from the parent tree. This ensures that different varieties of trees are scattered throughout the rainforest.

Pigs in the woods

Wild pigs are found in rainforests around the world. They root, or dig, in the soil with their snouts for their food and will eat plant roots, insects, and small animals. Pig herds can be very territorial and will attack other animals that stray into their territory, including unwary human travelers.

South American tapirs are nocturnal plant-eaters, meaning they feed at night.

ARCHITECTS OF THE RAINFOREST

African forest elephants are sometimes called "architects of the rainforest." They create clearings in the forest around drinking holes. These clearings can be 330 feet (100 m) or more across. Young plants have a difficult time establishing themselves because the elephants trample or eat them. Asian elephants play a similar role in the rainforests of India and Southeast Asia.

Understory Life

The understory isn't quite as dark as the forest floor, but it is still fairly dim. This level of the forest is made up of smaller trees, shrubs, and vines.

Understory trees have special adaptations that allow them to thrive in dim light. Some trees grow flowers directly on their trunks, making them easier to spot by pollinating birds and insects. The flowers will often have strong scents as well to attract pollinators.

Forest disguises

While it is important for tree flowers to be easily seen, rainforest animals often have adaptations that keep them hidden. Most of

HOME RAINFOREST

Many plants from the understory, such as zebra plants, are now common houseplants. Because they need very little sunlight or water, understory plants are well-suited to life in people's homes.

The green coloring of the parrot snake camouflages it as it hunts for frogs in the trees of the Amazon rainforest.

The South American red-eyed tree frog clings securely to the leaves and branches of the trees.

the **reptiles** that live in the understory are **camouflaged** to blend in with the background. The emerald tree boa's bright green color, for example, makes it difficult for eagles to see against the tree leaves. The disguise also helps the boa sneak up unseen on unsuspecting animals.

Larger animals can be hard to see in the forest, too. The jaguar's spots camouflage it in the dappled light falling through the leaves.

Forest frogs

The damp conditions of the understory are just right for **amphibians** such as salamanders and frogs. Amphibians need water to lay their eggs in and to keep their skin from drying out. Tree frogs' feet have tiny suction pads covered with a sticky

NOT SO FAST!

The three-toed sloth is very well adapted to life in the branches of the South American rainforest. It avoids drawing the attention of predators such as the jaguar by moving so slowly that it isn't noticed. It is also well disguised, thanks to a simple green plant, called an alga, that lives in its fur, making the brown sloth appear green!

substance. This adaptation helps them grip tree branches and move swiftly to escape **predators**.

15

Top of the Trees

The canopy, or overstory, of the rainforest is formed by a nearly continuous layer of tree crowns. It is a mysterious place, hard to reach, and full of life. The canopy varies from forest to forest. South America's forest treetops are bound together by plants and vines; African forest canopies are umbrella-shaped; and Asian forest trees have narrow crowns.

Dazzling diversity

There are a tremendous variety of living things in the rainforest habitat. About 9/10ths of the living things in the rainforest are found in the canopy. Some scientists believe that half of the world's animal species live in rainforest canopies.

The sun shines brightest in the canopy. Vines, trees, and other plants compete for the light. Because there is such an abundance of flowers and fruits and leaves, there is a great deal to eat in the canopy. With so many layers of plants on which to

The toucan is one of the many birds of the rainforest canopy. Its colorful beak is used to peel fruit and to catch young birds and insects.

Sugar glider females carry their young in pouches.

skin flap that stretches from their front to hind feet. Their sharp claws also make them excellent climbers. Another glider is the flying squirrel. There are more than 40 different types of flying squirrels, and many live in the world's rainforests. They can glide more than 160 feet (50 m) between trees. There are even flying frogs! They leap from tree to tree, spreading apart their long, webbed toes to glide through the air for 50 feet (15 m) or so.

swing, climb, and scurry, animals can spend their whole lives in the treetops and never touch the ground. There are frogs, for example, that breed in pools of water that collect in plants growing on the trees.

Animals that can fly are perfectly adapted for treetop life. Birds, bats, and, of course, insects are abundant in the canopy. Climbing animals, such as monkeys, squirrels, and lizards, are also present in large numbers.

Gliders

Some animals can't quite fly from tree to tree, but they can glide. One such animal is the sugar glider, found in the rainforests of New Guinea, Indonesia, and Australia. These tiny animals are a type of possum. They glide through the trees on a sail-like

CANOPY SHYNESS

Canopy trees in a rainforest do not actually touch one another. There are gaps between the trees, like the spaces between pieces in a mosaic. This is known as "canopy shyness," and no one knows exactly why it happens.

Tree Climbers

Not all of the plants that climb toward the light in the forest are trees or shrubs. Many plants use the trees against which they're competing for light to their advantage, relying on them for support. These highly adapted plants are found only in rainforests.

Lianas

Lianas often start out as shrubs, firmly rooted in the forest floor. As they grow, they put out long branches that attach themselves to the trunks of nearby trees or to tree saplings. The lianas and the trees climb together until they reach the sunlight at the roof of the forest. There the lianas produce large crowns of leaves and flowers. Almost half of the leaves in the forest canopy belong to lianas rather than trees. Lianas often produce **aerial roots**, which can absorb moisture from the air.

Epiphytes

Epiphytes are another type of plant that relies on trees for support. Unlike lianas, however, they are not rooted in the ground. Instead, they grow on tree trunks or in the crooks of branches. Epiphytes do not take any nutrients from the host tree, which only provides them with a place to grow. They have small, sticky roots that help them grip the tree. Some rely almost entirely on collecting rainwater as a source of minerals. Bromeliads, such as the pineapple plant, form a cup-shaped rosette of thick, waxy, waterproof leaves that can store more than eight gallons (30 l) of water. Many types of orchids and ferns are epiphytes.

◀ *Lianas are woody climbers that cling to the rainforest trees with long, hooked branches.*

▲ *Orchids are the most common type of epiphyte—plants that grow on other plants.*

Stranglers

Some epiphytes eventually become stranglers. At a certain point in their growth, they produce aerial roots that wrap around the trunk of the tree as they make their way down toward the ground. The increased supply of nutrients the plant gets in this way allows it to grow more strongly, and its branches soon spread upward into the canopy, competing with the tree for sunlight. Eventually, the strangler's roots completely surround the tree and kill it. When the dead tree trunk collapses, the strangler's strong network of roots—stretching from the canopy to the forest floor—continues to support the plant.

Monkeying Around

One of the most common inhabitants of the rainforest canopy is monkeys. They are superbly adapted to forest life, moving confidently through the branches and feasting on fruits, nuts, leaves, and berries.

New World monkeys

Monkeys are divided into two groups, according to which part of the world they live in. Old World monkeys are found in Africa and Asia. New World monkeys live in Central and South America.

Most New World monkeys belong to a family that includes the squirrel, spider, woolly, and capuchin monkeys. New World monkeys are found everywhere in the rainforest, from the forest floor to the top of the canopy. Most are fairly large. The largest, the woolly spider monkey, weighs more than 30 pounds (15 kg). Many New

World monkeys are very sociable. The squirrel monkey, for example, roams the trees in troops of up to 500 monkeys.

Tamarins and marmosets also belong to the New World monkey group. They are

The howler monkey has an extraordinarily loud call that can be heard several miles away.

"HOWL" LOUD IS THAT?

The howler monkey is one of the largest New World monkeys. Howlers defend their territories in the forest canopy by producing extraordinarily loud, deep, throaty calls. A howler chorus can be heard more than three miles (5 km) away.

▲ *The langurs of Asia are among the largest of the Old World monkeys.*

small monkeys; some are about the size of house cats, while others are no bigger than rats. Their tails are often longer than the rest of their bodies. Marmosets leap with great agility between tree branches, whereas tamarins tend to climb straight up and down.

Prehensile tails

Many New World monkeys have strong tails that on the underside are mostly hairless and covered with touch-sensitive pads. Monkeys use these specialized appendages, called **prehensile tails**, like an extra limb to grip branches when they are climbing through the trees.

Old World monkeys

Some types of Old World monkeys are found in tropical rainforests, but others live in grasslands and even in mountainous areas. Typical Old World rainforest monkeys include the colobus monkeys of Africa, and the macaques and langurs of Asia. Most are quite big, about the size of an average dog. The Hanuman langur, for example, has a three-foot-long (1 m) body. Many have cheek pouches for storing food that expand like a hamster's. This is a handy adaptation for monkeys that compete against each other for food and don't like to share. No New World monkeys have pouches, just as no Old World monkeys have a prehensile tail.

Apes of the Forest

The apes are humans' closest relatives in the animal world. The great apes include the chimpanzee, the bonobo, and gorilla of Africa, and the orangutan of Indonesia. Gibbons, found in Southeast Asia and Indonesia, are smaller and sometimes called the lesser apes.

The orangutans of Indonesia are highly intelligent animals as well as agile climbers.

Orangutans

The word "orangutan" means "man of the forest" in the language of Malasia and Indonesia. These great apes are found in a range of forest habitats on the islands of Borneo and Sumatra. Full-grown male orangutans can weigh around 220 pounds (100 kg). Female orangutans are much smaller.

Orangutans have a widely varied diet that includes leaves, bark, flowers, fruit, ants, termites, and birds' eggs. Big though they are, orangutans spend most of their time in the trees, swinging effortlessly on their long, powerful arms. Each night they make a fresh nest, complete with roof, in a tree.

Chimpanzees and bonobos

Chimpanzees are found in the forests and grasslands of equatorial Africa. Male chimpanzees weigh about 175 pounds (80 kg) and stand about three feet (1 m) tall; females are smaller.

Long-armed gibbons swing with ease from branch to branch in the forest.

Bonobos, or pygmy chimpanzees, are found in central Africa. They look very much like chimpanzees, except they are shorter, and have longer limbs and a more upright posture. Bonobos have black coats and shiny black faces. Bonobos and chimpanzees both build nests in trees for sleeping each night. Both will eat just about anything they can get their hands on, including honey, leaves, fruit, ants, birds' eggs, birds, smaller mammals, and reptiles.

Gorillas

Gorillas live in the forests of equatorial Africa. A full-grown male gorilla can weigh 330 pounds (150 kg) or more. Females are usually smaller. Adult males are often called silverbacks because as they get older, the hair on their backs turns from black to silver. But despite their size, gorillas are shy animals, living in small groups of 5 to 15 with one silverback leader. Gorillas eat plants, berries, and leaves each day. At night, gorillas build a camp, where the group sleeps. Females and their young make nests in the tree branches, while the males sleep under the tree.

Gibbons

Gibbons are the real kings of the swingers, moving with ease from branch to branch on their long, slim arms. They are the smallest of the ape family and are found in the forests of Southeast Asia and Indonesia. Pairs of gibbons often sing bird-like warbling duets in the morning.

A Multitude of Minibeasts

One of the things all rainforests around the world have in common is the countless insects and other minibeasts that crawl, scuttle, walk, and fly through every part of the forest.

Bugs in their billions

There are probably more than 50 million different types of insects and other minibeasts living in rainforests. A single rainforest tree might be home to more than 1,200 different kinds of beetles!

Minibeasts help keep the forest healthy. In the soil, earthworms, termites, and other tiny animals feed on the remains of plants, breaking them down into small particles that can be recycled by bacteria and fungi. Countless colorful butterflies fly through the forest air, playing a vital role as plant pollinators.

▼ *Although they have been known to catch and eat small birds, most giant spiders live on grasshoppers and other insects.*

Rainforest centipedes are powerful enough to take on frogs and lizards.

Big bugs

In the rainforest, some minibeasts tend to be a bit more maxi! Beetles in the forests of South America may reach six inches (16 cm) in length. Rainforest centipedes eight inches (20 cm) long kill their prey with poisonous claws that can inflict a nasty bite on the unwary human explorer, too. Hairy bird-eating spiders of South America can measure 10 inches (25 cm) across.

Ant antics

The animal that really deserves to be treated with respect in the rainforest is the ant—and there are an awful lot of them! Rainforest ants have ferociously painful bites and stings.

Leafcutter ants are common in rainforests around the world. **Foraging** parties of ants snip out bits of leaves with their strong jaws and then carry them back to their nests. Foraging ants are protected by soldier ants that may weigh 300 times more than them. Even tinier leafcutters ride on top of the leaves, keeping an eye out for flies that may lay eggs on the leafcutters' leaves.

NOW YOU SEE IT . . .
Many rainforest insects have incredible camouflage that allows them to hide from other animals—animals that may try to eat them. There are insects that look like dead leaves, living leaves, half-eaten leaves, twigs, bark, and flower parts.

Hunters of the Forest

Because large **prey** animals are scarce in the rainforest, large predators are naturally scarce, too. However, the ones that are found there are among the most spectacular in the world.

Top cats

The biggest hunters prowling the forest floor are cats. Asia has the tiger, South America the jaguar, and Africa the leopard. All of these cats are formidable hunters. Because large prey animals are often hard to find, the cats are specially adapted to eat smaller ones. The jaguar, for example, is an excellent swimmer and skilled at catching fish. It will also eat frogs and turtles.

The rainforest is also home to smaller cats such as the margay and ocelot of South America and the leopard cat of Asia. These animals are generally not much bigger than a house cat or dog. Most hunt at night, both on the forest floor and up in the canopy.

Civet cats

The most well-known member of the family of small, catlike hunters called civet cats is the mongoose. There are several different types of mongooses found in a variety of habitats

Tigers are the top predators in the rainforests of India.

across Africa, the Middle East, and India. They will eat snakes, small mammals, birds, and insects. They can crack eggs open by banging them against rocks.

 The long-snouted sloth bear is found in India and Sri Lanka.

Another interesting member of the civet cat family is the fishing genet. Although, as its name suggests, it likes fish, the genet is a poor swimmer and doesn't like to get wet. It will tap its paw on the surface of forest streams to attract fish. The genet lays its long, sensitive whiskers against the surface of the water. Only when it picks up the vibrations of a passing fish will it plunge swiftly into the water to make its catch.

Bears in the trees

Sloth bears are found in the tropical rainforests of Sri Lanka and southern India. They are among the most specialized of the bear family, as they are adapted for a life in the trees. The sloth bear is a large, black, shaggy animal. Its long, curved claws allow it to hang beneath branches like a real sloth. The sloth bear has a long snout, sensitive lips, and a long tongue. All of these adaptations help the sloth bear suck up its favorite meal—termites.

AERIAL HUNTER
The Philippine eagle, or "monkey-eating" eagle, is an awesome predator. It is roughly three feet (1 m) tall with a seven-foot (2 m) wingspan. Its long tail and broad wings are superbly adapted for swift flight among the trees. It has a massive, powerful beak and strong, clawed legs. Lemurs, squirrels, snakes, civet cats, bats, and even monkeys fall victim to this rainforest hunter.

The Threatened Forest

The amazing plants and wildlife of the rainforest are under threat. The danger to the world's rainforests comes from the activities of humans.

Removing trees from the rainforest for timber is incredibly destructive.

Deforestation

Deforestation is the destruction of a forest for timber or fuel, or to clear the land for agriculture. Although people argue about how fast the forests are disappearing, it is likely that at least 79,000 acres (32,000 ha) of forest disappear from Earth every day. This means that in 15 years an area the size of Mexico will have been lost. As the forest goes, so too do the animals that depend upon it. Many animals vanish into **extinction** without ever having been observed or named. As the forests are destroyed, more carbon dioxide, a **greenhouse gas**, is added to the air, possibly altering climates around the world.

As populations continue to grow, and cities get bigger, more pressure is put on the rainforest.

Farmers and ranchers

Poor farmers in rainforest countries can't afford to buy good farmland. Instead, they clear the rainforest to grow their crops. Ranchers also clear large areas of rainforest to make pastures for their cattle. Unfortunately, because most of the nutrients in a rainforest are stored in the trees, farmers soon find that the land they have cleared cannot support healthy growth. Within a few years, it will grow no more crops. So the farmers move on to another patch of forest and continue the cycle.

Logging

One of the biggest reasons for the destruction of the rainforests is its use as a source of **timber**. The heavy machinery used to build roads into the forest and to transport the timber causes a great deal of damage. Large areas of rainforest are destroyed to remove only a few logs. The heavy machinery compacts the soil, making it harder for new plants to grow. Because the rainforest trees are connected by a network of lianas and other climbers, cutting down one tree can bring down several more that are attached to it.

What can be done?

For the huge areas of rainforest that have already disappeared, it is too late. The plants and animals that have been lost can never be put back. But people around the world can help save what's left. Refraining from buying products made from rainforest hardwood trees, such as mahogany, is a start. Another way is to **boycott** pet stores that sell parrots, monkeys, and other endangered rainforest animals as pets. People need to recognize that rainforests are important to the whole world. **Developed countries** must provide financial assistance, education, or other kinds of help to poorer countries to help save the remaining forests. One idea might be to offer farmers low-cost loans that would allow them to buy non-rainforest land, and then promise to buy their products at a fair price. Only by working together will the world's people be able to protect the rainforests—Earth's priceless, living treasures.

Glossary

adaptation A characteristic of a living thing that allows it to survive in its environment; "drip tips", for example, are an adaptation that allows rainforest leaves to shed water.

aerial roots Roots that project from the above-ground part of a plant's stem.

altitude Height above the ground or sea level.

amphibians Types of animals, such as frogs and toads, with soft, moist skin, that spend at least part of their lives in water.

biomes Large areas of the environment with distinctive climates and plant types; examples include forests, mountains, and deserts.

boycott Refuse to buy or do something as a protest against it.

camouflaged Made difficult to see on account of being the same color or shape as something in the background.

canopy The topmost part of the forest trees; the "roof" of the forest.

compost Plant and animal remains that have been rotted down by the actions of minibeasts and microorganisms.

deforestation The clearance of trees from woods and forests for fuel or other purposes, or to clear the area for grazing or building.

developed countries Countries where the economy is based on industry rather than agriculture; the U.S. and Canada are developed countries.

equator An imaginary line that runs around the middle of the earth, dividing it into the northern and southern hemispheres.

equatorial Having to do with the equator.

evaporation The process by which a liquid changes into a vapor (or gas) without boiling; puddles of rainwater disappear as they evaporate in the sunshine.

extinction The disappearance of an entire species of living things from the world when the last members die.

fertile Able to support growth; fertile soil produces abundant plant growth.

foraging Searching for something to eat.

germinate Start to grow; when a seed grows and produces its first root and leaves, it has germinated.

greenhouse gas A type of gas in the atmosphere that traps heat as it rises from the surface of the earth, like the glass in a greenhouse, causing the atmosphere to be warmer than it would be if the heat escaped into space.

habitat The place where a living thing makes its home; the environment that it is adapted to survive in.

mammals Animals that are warm-blooded and usually have hair on their skins, including humans and monkeys; female mammals produce milk to feed their young.

nutrients Another word for food; all the things needed for a balanced diet to provide energy and raw materials for growth and maintenance of the organism.

pollinated When pollen grains have been carried to one flower from another it is said to have been pollinated; after this has happened, seeds will start to form.

predators Animals that catch and eat other animals for food.

prehensile tails Tails that can be used for grasping objects.

prey Animals that are caught and eaten by predators.

recycling Making waste materials available to be used again.

reptiles Cold-blooded animals, including snakes and lizards, with a dry, scaly skin; most lay soft-shelled eggs and live on land.

temperate climates Areas where the weather is rarely, if ever, extremely cold or extremely hot.

timber Wood that is used for building.

Index